D1403593

I Wonder Why Skunks Are So Smelly

mammals

-92
5,27

I Wonder
Why Skunks Are So Smelly

· · · · · · · · · · · · · · · ·

nd other neat facts about mammals

y Deborah De Ford
lustrated by Pedro Julio Gonzalez

c1

A GOLDEN BOOK • NEW YORK
Western Publishing Company, Inc., Racine, Wisconsin 53404

FORKED DEER
REGIONAL LIBRARY CENTER

Produced by Graymont Enterprises, Inc., Norfolk, Connecticut
Producer: *Ruth Lerner Perle*
Design: *Michele Italiano-Perla*
Editorial consultant: *Penny Kalk*, New York Zoological Society, Bronx, New York

© 1992 Graymont Enterprises, Inc. All rights reserved. Printed in the U.S.A. No part of this book may be copied or reproduced in any form without written permission from the publisher. All trademarks are the property of Western Publishing Company, Inc. Library of Congress Catalog Card Number: 91-75921
ISBN: 0-307-11323-X/ISBN: 0-307-61323-2 (lib. bdg.)   A   MCMXCII

Contents

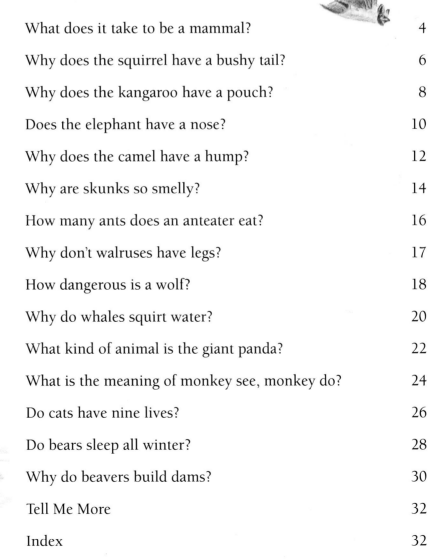

What does it take to be a mammal?

Giraffes, chipmunks, zebras, seals, deer, hippopotamuses, bats, dogs, walruses, pigs, and seals are all mammals.

Mammals may be as huge as whales, tiny as mice, fast as cheetahs, or slow as sloths. They may live in jungles, on icebergs, underwater, on mountaintops, in deserts, or in your backyard. They may be *herbivores*, eating only plants; *carnivores*, eating only meat; or, like human beings, *omnivores*, eating meat, fruits, plants, and vegetables.

But no matter how different mammals may be from one another, there are some things about them that are the same.

What makes an animal a mammal?

It is hairy. All or some of its body is covered with hair, fur, wool, bristles, spines or quills.

It gives birth to live babies and feeds them mother's milk. (Except the duck-bill platypus and the spiny anteater, which lay eggs.)

It is a vertebrate. That means it has a backbone and a bony skeleton inside its body.

It is warm-blooded. Its body temperature stays about the same, no matter what the outside temperature may be.

It has no more than four limbs. The limbs may be arms, legs, flippers, wings, or fins.

It uses lungs to breathe, taking oxygen out of the air and expelling carbon dioxide.

Is a dolphin a fish?

No. Dolphins are sea mammals. They are shaped like fish and live in the water, but they don't have gills. Instead, they have lungs and must come to the surface of the water to breathe air. Unlike fish, they are warm-blooded, and the females have special glands that produce milk for their newborn babies.

Is an armadillo a reptile?

No. An armadillo resembles a reptile because it looks as if it has horny scales. But its "scales" are really ridges of bone covered with skin. Unlike reptiles, armadillos are warm-blooded and have some hair on the underside of their bodies, so they, too, are mammals.

Is a bat a bird?

No. A bat is the only mammal that has wings and can fly like a bird. But unlike a bird's, a bat's body is covered with fur, not feathers. Like other mammals, it gives birth to live babies that nurse on mother's milk.

What furry-looking animal is not a mammal?

A penguin looks like a mammal because it appears to be furry. But that "fur" is really a coat of tightly knit feathers. Unlike mammals, penguins hatch from eggs and are not nursed by their mothers.

Why does the squirrel have a bushy tail?

Most squirrels have beautiful bushy tails. But their tails are more than just beautiful. Squirrels put their wonderful tails to many good uses. A squirrel's all-purpose tail is:

a balancing pole

Squirrels use their tails for balance as they scamper up trees and across branches.

a signal sender

By fluffing and flicking their tails, squirrels let each other know how they feel or when danger is near.

a blanket

Squirrels that live where winter occurs wrap themselves in their tails to keep warm.

a parasol

Where the weather is hot, squirrels hold their tails over their backs to shield themselves from the sun.

Can squirrels really fly?

The flying squirrel has furry flaps of skin that connect the front and back legs on each side of its body. As it leaps from tree to tree, it stretches its legs wide so the skin flaps catch the air. Its tail helps it keep its balance and steer.

Deep sleep

If they live where the winter is cold, some squirrels crawl into ground holes, hollow trees, or empty birds' nests. They curl into a little ball, with their noses to their bellies and their tails wrapped tightly around their bodies. They can go without eating for months at a time.

Where do squirrels get food in winter?

During the fall months, squirrels prepare for winter by gathering acorns and nuts. They eat as many as they can, and store the rest in secret hiding places so they'll have food during winter.

Amazing but TRUE

Ground squirrels build long tunnels underground where they live and hide. They often live together in groups and take turns watching for danger. The lookout squirrel stands on its hind legs at the entrance to the tunnel. If it spots trouble, it whistles to warn the other squirrels.

Chew, chew, chew

A squirrel's front teeth are sharp and strong enough to gnaw through nut shells, roots, and tree bark. These teeth never wear out because they keep growing throughout the squirrel's life.

Why does the kangaroo have a pouch?

The female kangaroo has a pocket, or pouch, at the front of her body that is specially designed to carry newborn kangaroos. Most mammal babies walk and run just a few days after they are born. But the baby kangaroo, or *joey*, is about the size of a lima bean when it is born and cannot manage by itself.

As soon as the joey is born, it climbs up its mother's belly and into the pouch, where it finds a supply of milk. The fur-lined pouch keeps the little one warm and safe. After about six months, the joey is big and strong enough to leave the pouch and hop around by itself.

How far can kangaroos hop?

No animal on earth can hop as far as a big kangaroo. It can leap a distance of twenty-five or more feet in a single hop. That's about the width of a tennis court. Both big red and gray kangaroos can hop faster than most horses can run. Their long, strong hind legs and thick tails give them the power and balance they need for fast hopping. Females, called *does*, hop faster than the larger males, called *boomers*.

Tell Me More

Kangaroos are herbivores, and so they travel from place to place looking for grass and leaves to eat. When they get tired, they just sit back and balance themselves on their hind legs and tails.

A kangaroo licks its paws when it feels too warm. As its paws dry, the moisture evaporates and the kangaroo feels cooler.

Does the elephant have a nose?

The elephant has the longest, strongest, most amazing nose in the world—its trunk, which is really its upper lip and nose together. Like other noses, the elephant's trunk has two nostrils for breathing and smelling. But that long, wrinkly, swinging trunk does much more than nose work!

Elephants use their trunks like loud-speakers to make their sounds heard. They can grumble, grunt, scream, and trumpet to tell their friends how they feel.

The trunk is also handy for:

Picking
One or two knobs on the end of the elephant's trunk act as delicate fingers with which it can pull blades of grass or pick up objects as small as a berry.

What are tusks?

Tusks are large ivory teeth that stick out of the elephant's mouth. The elephant uses its tusks to strip the bark off trees—its favorite food. Its tusks are important tools for lifting things, for digging, and for fighting.

Showering
Sometimes the elephant sucks water into its trunk and then turns it into a shower spray.

Drinking
The elephant uses its trunk like a giant straw to suck up gallons of water. Then the elephant turns the trunk into a hose and squirts the water into its mouth.

Lifting, pulling, reaching
Using its strong and flexible trunk, the elephant can uproot a tree, lift heavy logs, or pull leaves from a branch high above its head.

Hugging
The female elephant uses her trunk like an arm to hug her babies and guide them gently along a path. Two grown elephants may wrap their trunks together as a sign of friendship.

Snorkeling
When the elephant bathes in deep water, it keeps its trunk high and dry above the surface, allowing the animal to breathe while the rest of its body is submerged.

Amazing
but TRUE

Baby elephants may be big, but they are still babies. A baby elephant sometimes sucks its trunk the way a human baby sucks its thumb!

Why does the camel have a hump?

The camel's hump is like a built-in backpack for storing extra fat. When the camel can't find food in the dry, hot desert, it uses the fat in its hump to keep from going hungry.

When the camel has used up the fat in its hump, the hump flops over or slides to one side of its body, just like an empty sack.

How can camels survive in the desert?

The camel's body is perfectly designed for living in the sand, wind, and sun of the desert. Besides its hump, which also protects its back from the sun's heat, the camel has other marvelous body parts:

Fancy feet

The camel's feet are equipped with thick pads and two large toes that spread out flat so it can easily walk or run without sinking into the sand.

Desert shields

The camel has broad ridges of bone over each eye that shield its eyes from the sun.

The eyes have it, have it, have it

Three sets of eyelids protect the camel's eyes from sandstorms. Two of its lids are fringed with long, bushy lashes that keep the sand out. The third lid is transparent and comes down like a window shade to wipe the camel's eyes clean.

The nose knows

The camel has nose muscles that can close its long, narrow nostrils when the sand starts to blow.

Mighty mouth

The camel's mouth is tough enough to eat spiny cacti and other rough desert plants.

Are camels ever thirsty?

Camels can go without water for months if they have to. They don't carry extra water in their bodies. But they can stand extreme heat without sweating and losing water.

Sooner or later, though, even camels need a drink of water. The longer they go without water, the more they drink when they finally find a watering place.

Temper, temper

Camels are easily annoyed, and may bite, spit, or kick when they get angry. Sometimes they don't react right away, but they do hold grudges and show their annoyance eventually.

Amazing but TRUE

The male camel has an extra piece of pink skin in his mouth. When he wants to frighten or impress another camel, he fills the skin with air and blows it out of his mouth like a balloon. The camel adds to the effect by making a roaring sound.

Why are skunks so smelly?

Skunks, like all animals, need a way to protect themselves. Fast animals can run or swim away from danger. Strong animals can fight their enemies with teeth, claws, or beaks. A skunk is neither fast nor strong, but its body has a different weapon.

Two glands near the skunk's tail make an oily yellow liquid that has a terrible odor. When the skunk is in danger, it sprays this liquid at its enemy.

Anyone who has been sprayed by a skunk is unlikely to forget it. When most animals see the striped critter ambling fearlessly along, they run for cover, or at least step carefully out of its path. Even a big black bear runs when it sees a skunk.

Look out!

Skunks have different ways of warning their enemies before they spray. Sometimes a skunk will hold its tail up like a flag. Sometimes it will make hissing sounds and stamp the ground with its front paws.

The spotted skunk raises its whole tail end and balances on its front paws in a kind of handstand. But no matter what warnings skunks use, they always mean the same thing: "Go away and leave me alone before it's too late!"

Does any animal fight the skunk?

The horned owl isn't frightened by the skunk's smell. It swoops silently down in the night and grabs the skunk with its sharp talons. The awful smell remains on the owl's feathers long after dinner is over.

Even though the skunk's sprayers are located at its back end, it still has almost perfect aim. A skunk can spray an animal in the face from ten feet away!

What do skunks eat?

Skunks are omnivores that feed on fruits, worms, insects, fish, and small animals. Some even eat rattlesnakes!

Amazing *but* TRUE

The odor of a skunk's spray is so strong that it can sometimes stop its victims from breathing.

14

How many ants does an anteater eat?

The giant anteater is one of the strangest creatures in the Amazon rainforest. It's remarkable that such a large animal eats nothing but ants and termites. To get enough nourishment, the anteater must eat thousands and thousands of insects a day.

Anteaters have no teeth. They just lap up their prey and swallow.

Snappy snout

The anteater's long, narrow snout is just the right shape for reaching into termite nests. Its tiny mouth is less than a half inch wide, but it is wide enough for its long, sticky tongue to dart out and capture tiny insects.

When an anteater feels threatened by a wildcat or other predator, it stands upright on its hind legs and holds out its claws as if to say: "Think twice before you come near me!"

Bringing up baby

Baby anteaters often ride on their mother's back and hide under her long, woolly fur. They use their tiny claws to hold tight, and they remain safely attached to her even when she runs.

Clever claws

The huge claws on the anteater's front paws are useful for scratching holes in termite nests, but they get in the way when the anteater walks, so the anteater tucks its claws under and walks on its knuckles.

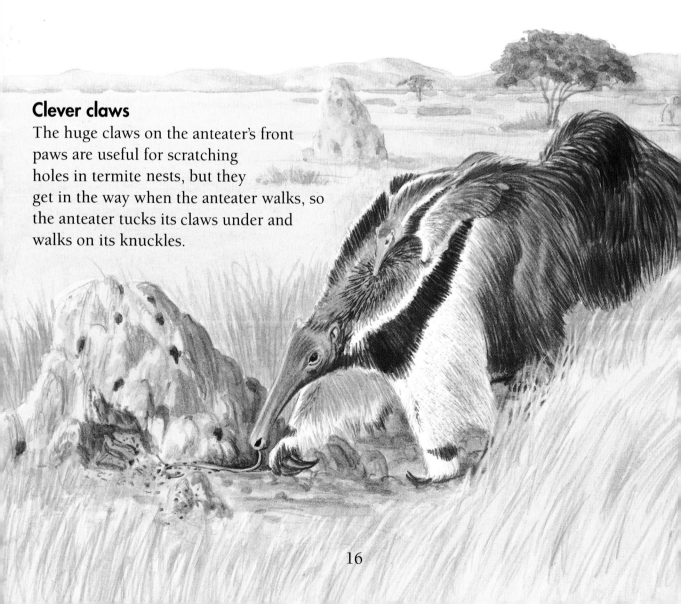

Why don't walruses have legs?

Walruses and their cousins, seals and sea lions, are marine mammals called *pinnipeds*—a group of animals that spend much of their time in the water and thus have flippers instead of legs and arms. These flippers are perfect for swimming, though they make moving around on land difficult. But walruses have something the other pinnipeds don't have: Both males and females have long, strong tusks that never stop growing.

These tusks are perfectly shaped for clam digging and for transferring food into the animal's mouth.

Amazing
but TRUE

Male walruses have big pouches around their necks. They can fill them with air until they are as big as basketballs. These pouches act like life preservers and help the animals float in the water.

Why do walruses have whiskers?

Walruses use their sensitive face whiskers to find shellfish on the ocean floor.

Tell Me More

Female walruses give birth to their young on land. When the babies are big enough, the mothers hold them between their front flippers and take them swimming.

17

How dangerous is a wolf?

Wolves are the ancestors of man's best friend—the dog. All dogs, large and small, belong to the same family as wolves—the *canine* family. Like dogs, wolves are very intelligent, loyal to their fellow wolves, friendly, and playful. They wag their tails to show they are happy and lick each other to show affection. And, like dogs, wolves are carnivores. They hunt for animals, but they hardly ever attack people. When wolves get very hungry, they may attack sheep or weak cows, and so ranchers and farmers consider them trouble. That may be where their bad reputation started.

What is a pack of wolves?

Wolves live together in groups called packs. As a rule, the members of a pack are part of one family. They protect one another, hunt together, and share in the work of raising their pups. Once a wolf has found a mate, the two stay together as long as they live. Most pups stay with their parents and their pack.

18

How do wolves hunt?

Individual wolves hunt for small animals, but the pack works together to surprise and kill a large animal, such as a deer. When the wolves spot their prey, they set off in single file behind their leader. They surround the animal and try to confuse it into running away. When it runs off, the wolves attack it from all sides.

Follow the leader

The largest, strongest male is usually the leader of the pack. Males fight each other to see who is the strongest. When a leader emerges, the other members of the pack must go where he leads and do as he directs. To show their loyalty to the leader, they crouch, flatten their ears, and tuck their tails between their legs.

Why do wolves howl?

In the quiet of night, a lone wolf howl may suddenly be heard. Soon another howl joins the first. Then another and another. Wolves usually howl to keep in touch or find one another when they are lost. The howlers may be protecting new pups or guarding a fresh kill. The howling also sends a clear message that tells other packs to stay away.

You can tell how important a wolf is within the pack by the way it holds its tail. The higher its rank, the higher it holds its tail.

Why do whales squirt water?

Whales and also dolphins, their smaller relatives, have something that no other mammals have: two blowholes at the top of their heads. These holes are nostrils through which whales breathe. The whale comes to the surface of the water to take in air through its blowholes. When it goes underwater again, the blowholes close.

After about ten minutes, the whale comes up again. But before it takes another breath, it blows out the old air through its blowholes. This creates a spray of water that looks like a fountain.

What makes whales so special?

Of all the amazing animals on earth, whales are the most astounding. They spend their whole lives in the water, but they are not fish. They are warm-blooded, but they have neither hair nor fur to keep them warm. Though they look like prehistoric monsters, most are the gentlest of creatures.

How do whales stay warm?

Except for some brushlike hair on their heads, whales have no hair or fur like other mammals. Instead, they have a thick layer of fatty tissue called *blubber* under their skin. The blubber acts like a blanket, keeping their body heat in and the cold out.

The blue whale—a gentle giant

The blue whale is the largest and heaviest animal on earth. The largest elephant looks tiny compared to a blue whale, which is about a hundred feet long and weighs as much as four hundred thousand pounds! That's as long as three city buses and as heavy as two thousand compact cars. A newborn blue whale weighs six thousand pounds.

How does a blue whale eat without teeth?

The largest animal on earth has no teeth! Instead, it has hundreds of long, thin bony plates of *baleen*, or whalebone, suspended from the roof of its mouth. These plates form a kind of strainer. With its huge mouth wide open, the blue whale swims through a school of tiny shrimplike animals called *krill*. When the whale has scooped up a huge mouthful of krill, it snaps its mouth shut. The water runs out, and the little animals are trapped inside. All the whale then has to do is gulp and swallow.

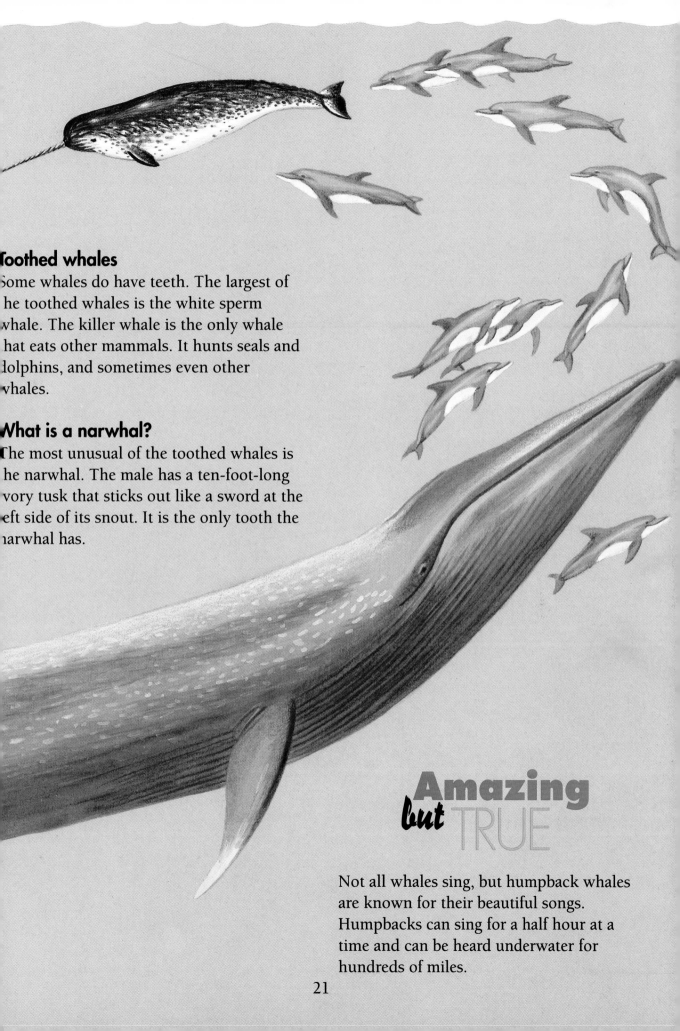

Toothed whales

Some whales do have teeth. The largest of the toothed whales is the white sperm whale. The killer whale is the only whale that eats other mammals. It hunts seals and dolphins, and sometimes even other whales.

What is a narwhal?

The most unusual of the toothed whales is the narwhal. The male has a ten-foot-long ivory tusk that sticks out like a sword at the left side of its snout. It is the only tooth the narwhal has.

Amazing but TRUE

Not all whales sing, but humpback whales are known for their beautiful songs. Humpbacks can sing for a half hour at a time and can be heard underwater for hundreds of miles.

21

What kind of animal is the giant panda?

The giant panda is one of nature's mysteries. No one is absolutely sure to which group of animals the giant panda belongs. We do know that giant pandas are *not* giants, since most are no more than five feet tall.

Is it a bear?

Like bears, giant pandas can walk on all four paws, or stand flat on their hind feet and walk upright for short distances. Pandas have a big round head and a body like a bear's. They can swim, climb, and stand on their head, as many bears do.

Is it a raccoon?

The little red panda is the giant panda's cousin. It has a red coat, striped face, and bushy ringed tail. Its face markings look like the giant panda's. Both animals live in the mountains of China and Tibet and eat bamboo in the same way. The red panda is considered a raccoon.

What makes the giant panda special?

The giant panda is the only mammal that can touch its head to the bottom of its foot. Unlike the bear and raccoon, the giant panda can use its wrists like a thumb for grasping, and it can sit down when it eats.

What do giant pandas eat?

Bamboo is the most important source of food for giant pandas. If bamboo ever disappeared, so would the giant panda.

Brrr

It can get very cold where the giant panda lives, but even when the ground is covered with snow, bamboo stays fresh and green. Giant pandas love the cold, so they wander happily through the snow, chomping bamboo as they go. They often slide down a snowy hillside on their stomach and then climb up and slide down again, just as children do when they go sledding.

Fun and games

In many ways giant pandas behave like people. They like to play and do somersaults, just for the fun of it. Sometimes they will suddenly stop moving and remain poised in a funny position.

The female giant panda carries her baby in her mouth, as a cat carries its kitten. At rest, she holds the baby with her front legs, cuddling it the way a human being cradles a baby.

What is the meaning of monkey see, monkey do?

Monkeys are intelligent and friendly, in many ways behaving like human beings. Monkeys are also great mimics. They copy what other monkeys do, and when they are around people, they copy what human beings do, too. Young monkeys learn by watching older monkeys. When an older monkey scampers up a tree, the young one follows close behind. If the first monkey grabs a banana, the second monkey does the same.

Here comes the groom

When it's time to clean up, monkeys use a friendly style of "dry cleaning." One monkey sits quietly while another monkey carefully picks the dirt, dry skin, and insects out of its fur. The monkeys take turns cleaning, or grooming, each other all day long. But this habit of constant combing and stroking does more than just keep them clean. Grooming each other seems to calm the monkeys and help them get along better.

How do monkeys swing by their tails?

Most monkeys have thumbs on their hands and feet. That's how they can hook their hands around branches. Some monkeys have another way of swinging through the trees: by their *prehensile* tails—tails that can curl around things and grasp them.

Tell Me More

onkeys are *primates*—animals that have
ng arms and legs and large hands and
et. Primates have thumbs that make it
sy to hold things. Most have fingers and
t nails instead of claws. Apes and human
ings are also primates.

Amazing but TRUE

o two monkeys' fingers are the same. Each
monkey has a set of its own fingerprints,
which are different from those of any
ther monkey!

Do cats have nine lives?

Cats don't really have more than one life, but they certainly seem to survive a lot of danger. Domestic cats have fallen off high rooftops, landed on all four feet, and then walked away without a twitch of their whiskers.

But if domestic cats have exciting lives, imagine the lives of cats in the wild! There are more than thirty kinds of wild cats, but the big cats are by far the most spectacular.

The big cats

Lions, tigers, leopards, and jaguars are known as the big cats. Most live in jungles or forests, but some live in deserts or even in the snow.

Leopards and jaguars

Leopards are known for their spots. Like the tiger's stripes, their spots help to disguise them. Snow leopards have lighter coloring that blends in with their snowy surroundings. A leopard is so strong that it can drag a captured animal twice its size up a tree. Jaguars hunt both on land and in the water. They eat monkeys, deer, frogs, snakes, turtles, birds, fish, and even crocodiles.

Tigers

The tiger is the largest of all the cats. Its striped coat blends in with jungle growth, so it can stalk and pounce on its prey without being seen. Tigers that live in snowy regions have longer fur and lighter markings than jungle tigers have. The markings on the tiger's face are like fingerprints—no two patterns are alike.

26

Amazing *but* TRUE

In ancient Egypt, people worshiped cats. When a cat died, its owners would wrap it in cloth and make a mummy out of it. They gave each dead cat mice mummies to take along into its next life.

Lions

Most famous of all the cats is the mighty lion, king of beasts. Lions have tawny coats, as well as tufts at the end of their tails. The males have great hairy manes framing their heads. Lions are the only cats that live in family groups called *prides*. Lion cubs have spots when they are born, but lose them as they get older.

Whether they are wild or tame, big or small, cats are all good hunters. They walk noiselessly on the pads of their feet while stalking their prey, then pounce and devour it.

All cats have:

keen eyes that see well in the dark.

keen ears that can perk up and turn in different directions.

sharp teeth with special fangs for capturing and killing their prey.

a sensitive nose that can sniff out prey at long distances.

whiskers to help them feel their way in the dark.

five toes on each of their front feet and **four** on each of their hind feet.

retractable claws that they can pull into their paws. (The cheetah is the exception, since it cannot retract its claws.)

a raspy tongue for licking bones clean and grooming their fur.

Do bears sleep all winter?

When the days grow cold and food gets scarce, most bears make themselves a winter home, or den, and go into a long deep sleep. They breathe more slowly, but not as slowly as a true hibernating animal. Females have their cubs in winter, so they stay in their dens almost all the time. But some males wake up and go out for a stroll on warmer days. Black bears sleep longer and deeper than most other bears.

How do black bears prepare for the winter?

In early fall, black bears prepare for their winter sleep. Since they are omnivores, they eat just about anything they can find— plants, berries, seeds, insects, honey, fish, and small mammals. When they are nice and fat, they look for a cozy den inside a cave or a hole in the ground. They line the den with leaves and branches and climb in as soon as it gets cold. Then they usually sleep until spring, when food is plentiful again.

Tell Me More

Bears walk flat on their feet, the way people do. When they stand up on their hind legs, they look almost like big children. That may be why stuffed bears are a favorite toy all over the world. But real bears are not to be toyed with! Black bears may look friendly, but they can attack when they are teased or hurt.

New arrivals

Black bear babies are born in the winter. The newborn cubs are blind, have hardly any hair, and weigh less than a half pound. But they drink plenty of their mother's rich milk and grow fast. By the time spring comes, the cubs have furry coats and have grown big and strong enough to leave the den and hunt and climb with their mother.

Amazing *but* TRUE

When bears eat too much honey, they get cavities in their teeth.

Why are polar bears white?

Polar bears live near the North Pole, where ice and snow cover the earth most of the year. Their light yellow fur blends in with the snow, so they can sneak up on an unsuspecting walrus or seal without being seen. Sometimes a polar bear covers its dark nose and mouth with its white paw to be sure it won't be spotted in the snow.

Polar bears make their dens by digging a hole in a snowbank, but they don't sleep there through the winter. The layer of fat under their skin, together with their thick fur coat, keeps them warm even in the icy Arctic wind and water. They can leave the den without fear of freezing.

Big brown bears

The brown bear is one of the largest and strongest meat-eating mammals on earth. One swat of its giant paw can bring down a deer or knock a fish out of the water.

29

Why do beavers build dams?

Of all mammals, beavers are the best and busiest architects and builders. They build their homes in water, which must be at least four feet deep so predators will stay away.

If the beavers can't find a river or stream that is deep enough, they use sticks, stones, and mud to make a wall, or dam, across the stream. The dam blocks the water and forms a nice deep pond. The deeper the beavers want the pond to be, the higher they build the dam.

Home sweet home

Once the water is deep enough, the beavers are ready to build their home, or lodge—a hollow mound, most of which is underwater. Underwater tunnels leading into the lodge allow the beavers to get in and out easily. A special area inside the lodge is built above the water so the beaver family can have a dry place to rest. This is where baby beavers are born during the spring.

How come beavers swim so well?

Beavers are built for swimming and can best escape their enemies when they are in the water. Their webbed hind feet make it easy for them to paddle, and their big flat tails make perfect rudders for steering.

When a beaver dives, its nose and ears close tight. Flaps of skin behind its teeth keep water out of its mouth and throat, and it can hold its breath underwater for about fifteen minutes. As added protection, an extra pair of see-through eyelids covers the beaver's eyes.

Tell Me More

When danger is near, the beaver raises its tail above the water and then slaps it down with a loud splash to scare its enemies and to warn other beavers.

hat big teeth you have!

e beavers' most valuable tools are their
th. When they build dams and lodges,
ey use their teeth to cut down hundreds
young trees. Then they chew off the
anches and twigs, split the trunks into
cks, and carry them to the pond. Of
urse, their teeth get worn down, but
t's no problem for the beavers. Their
nt cutting teeth never stop growing!

After beavers have cut down all the trees
close to their pond, they often travel far
from their home to find more trees. If the
trees are too far away to be carried, the
beavers dig a waterway, or canal, that leads
to their pond. Then they float the cut-up
trees down the canal to the pond.

Tell Me More

Though you have come to the last page of this book, you are only beginning to know about the wonderful true-life stories of mammals. Scientists who study mammals are called *mammalogists*. But you don't have to be a mammalogist to enjoy finding out more about these amazing members of the animal kingdom.

There seems to be a plan and a purpose for everything in nature. Large or small, beautiful or strange, each plant and animal has a role to fulfill. Each has an effect on something else that sooner or later has an effect on us.

Here are some more amazing-but-true facts to start you on your way to new discoveries:

• The four "big" cats—jaguars, leopards, tigers, and lions—cannot purr as all other cats can. Tigers and lions are the only cats that can roar. Lions can also meow.

• Elephants sleep only about three hours each night.

• The panda's skin is two-toned. It is light in places where its fur is white, and dark in places where its fur is black.

• Chimpanzees are three times stronger than people.

• So many wolves have been killed by people that there are hardly any of these animals left in the United States.

• Bats usually hunt at night. They find their way in the dark by using their ears—not their eyes. A bat sends out high-pitched squeaks that human beings can't hear. When these sounds reach something in the bat's path, such as an insect, the sounds bounce back like an echo, and the bat knows where to catch its prey. This system is similar to radar detection.